Owl Rescue

Written by
Carol Pugliano-Martin

Illustrated by
Elisabeth Bastian

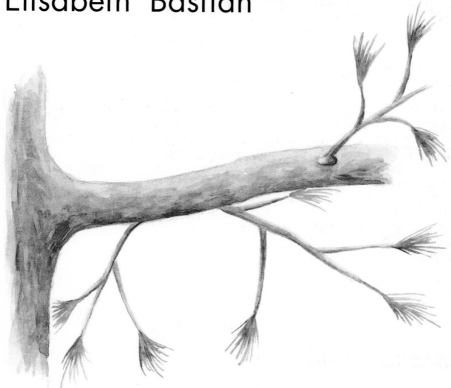

One day, my brother and I
found an owl in our yard.
His wing was hurt.

Dad called
the animal rescue center.

A worker from the center
came to get the owl.
Then we all went
to the center.

The vet put a bandage
on the wing.

"What's that for?" I asked.

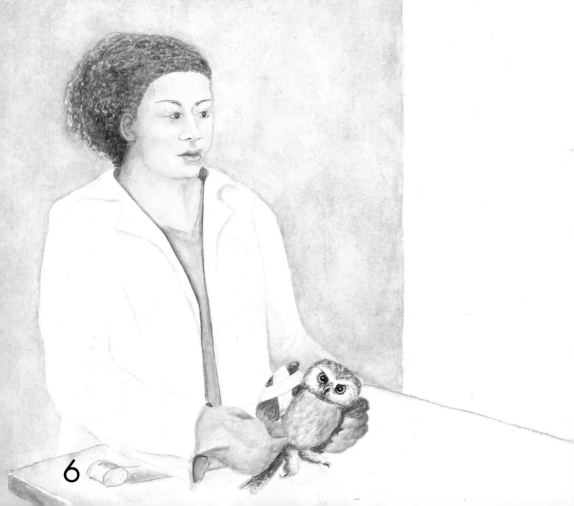

"This will help the wing get better," she said.

Then she gave the owl
some drops.

"What's that for?" I asked.

"This will make the owl
feel better," she said.

She put the owl in a pen.
She gave him food
and water.

We went to see the owl
every week.

One day, the owl
flew around his pen.
He was ready
to leave the center.

13

The worker brought him
back to our yard.
Then she let him go.

"Good-bye, little owl,"
I called out.

The owl flew off
into the tree.
The next morning,
he was gone.